BALLSBRIDGE THEN & NOW

HUGH ORAM

First published 2012

The History Press Ireland
119 Lower Baggot Street
Dublin 2
Ireland
www.thehistorypress.ie

British Library Cataloguing in Publication Data.
A catalogue record for this book is available from the British Library.

ISBN 978 1 84588 726 1

Typesetting and origination by The History Press
Printed in India
Manufacturing managed by Jellyfish Print Solutions Ltd

CONTENTS

ACKNOWLEDGEMENTS

I should especially like to thank John Holohan, chairman of the Ballsbridge, Donnybrook and Sandymount Historical Association, Brian Siggins, historian, and Gerard Whelan, librarian, RDS, for providing photographs for this book. Gerry Downey, Pat Murray and Anthony Harrison gave much help in the preparation of the work, as did Pat Herbert of the Hurdy Gurdy Wireless Museum in Howth and David Crampton of G. & T. Crampton. Dr David O'Donoghue helped with his reminiscences and photographs of Upper Baggot Street, which were prepared for a meeting of the Pembroke Road Residents' Association. Others who helped, in alphabetical order, were:

Baggot Street Wines, Bobby Barden, Robert Barklie, Anna-Maria Barry, Denis Bergin, Rachel Bewley-Bateman, Dan Bradley, Ruth Brennan, Peter Brittain, Paddy Burke (Burke's Pharmacy), Norman Campion, Chester Beatty Library, City of Dublin Vocational Education Committee, Dr Mary Clarke, Margot Collins (US Embassy), Mary Cosgrave, Austin Cromie, Kevin Dawson, Rose Donegan, Fred Duffy, Don Hall, Noelle Dowling, Colette Edwards (National Botanic Gardens/ OPW library), Alex Findlater, Grant's photo and print shop, Very Revd Monsignor Patrick Finn and the staff of the parish office staff of St Mary's church, OWP Hacketts, John Maiben Gilmartin, Val Joyce, David Kelly, Dermot Lacey, Angus Laverty (An Post), John Loughran, Helen Losty, Johnston, Mooney & O'Brien, Carla Marrinan (National Print Museum), Lisa McCarthy (Diageo), News Four, Maria McHugh, Claire McIlraith, Pierce Meagher, Fraser Mitchell, Derek Mooney (RTÉ), Gerry Moore, Hugh O'Byrne, Maeve Plower, John Ryan, Sinead Ward, Mandy Vaughan, Nicola Williams.

I should especially like to thank my wife Bernadette for her help, support and patience while I was researching and writing this book.

ABOUT THE AUTHOR

Hugh Oram is a media journalist, broadcaster and author who has lived in Ballsbridge for many years. He has been contributing to *The Irish Times* for over thirty years and has made many contributions over a similar time span to RTÉ Radio 1. He has also contributed on a wide variety of topics to many other newspapers, magazines, websites and radio stations, both in Ireland and beyond.

With books, he has made many contributions to international travel series published by Michelin, Paris; Random House, New York and Berlitz, USA, and has produced many Ireland guidebooks for Appletree Press in Belfast. He has written several company histories, including those of Bewley's, Weir's of Grafton Street, the K Club and Flahavan's, and has written many historical books on towns throughout Ireland. His most recently published in this genre was *Old Drogheda*.

INTRODUCTION

Until the mid-nineteenth century, virtually all of Ballsbridge was open country, and it wasn't until the 1850s and 1860s that the roads so closely connected with the district, such as Wellington Road, Clyde Road and Elgin Road, were built. The Pembroke Estate was crucial in much of this development. The Fitzwilliam family had settled in south Dublin in the mid-1300s and the 6th Viscount Fitzwilliam began the development of the Ballsbridge area in the mid-eighteenth century. The Pembroke Estate still exists but in a much reduced form.

Another vital element in the evolution of Ballsbridge was the establishment of the Pembroke Township in 1863. It lasted until 1930, when it was absorbed into Dublin Corporation.

One of the earliest developments to have had a vast impact on the district was the opening of the Westland Row to Kingstown railway line in 1834. Initially, the railway station at Lansdowne Road included 'Ballsbridge' in its name.

Ballsbridge has also seen the development of educational institutions, such as Marian College and the Ballsbridge College of Further Education, as well as the national school attached to St Mary's in Haddington Road. The old Pembroke School, popularly known as 'Miss Meredith's', is fondly remembered and a leading present-day school, St Conleth's in Clyde Road, started in that location just before the Second World War.

The district has also seen the establishment of some prime hotels, such as the old Jurys Hotel and the Berkeley Court Hotel, and is noted for its restaurants – its most famous being Roly's, which has been trading for the past twenty years.

Some amenities have disappeared due to development, such as the old botanic garden, but new facilities have greatly enhanced the life of the area, most notably the opening of the rugby stadium in Lansdowne Road in the early 1870s. It was a huge boost to the area, and these days the replacement Aviva stadium is a fine sporting arena, bringing countless visitors to Ballsbridge.

The biggest single development in Ballsbridge has been the expansion of the RDS in the district over more than 130 years. The RDS, founded in 1731, relocated to Ballsbridge after the foundation of the new Free State Government in 1922. The whole RDS site has been much enhanced in recent years and all the activities associated with the RDS, including the annual Horse Show and many exhibitions, ensure that it continues to play a pivotal role in Ballsbridge.

The district has seen many changes in employment. Two of the biggest employers are long since gone: Johnston, Mooney & O'Brien's bakery, which is now located in Finglas, and the old Irish Hospitals' Sweepstakes, which was replaced by the National Lottery.

The first new public building of major importance was the US Embassy, opened in 1964. The public initially abhorred the design, but now that the Embassy is likely to move many Ballsbridge residents will be sorry to see it go. Ballsbridge has seen many large-scale commercial developments, such as the AIB Bankcentre and the redevelopment of the Johnston, Mooney & O'Brien site.

Ballsbridge has been utterly transformed during its history, from a largely rural district, outside the city of Dublin, to a very modern and affluent suburb that's an integral part of the story of the modern city. Along the way, many changes and the contributions of many historical figures have combined to create the richness of its history.

JUNCTION OF ELGIN ROAD AND RAGLAN ROAD

THE SCENE AT this road junction has changed little over the past century, apart from the addition of traffic signs. Elgin Road was built in 1863/4 and named after the 8th Earl of Elgin (1811-63), whose appointments included Governor General of Canada and High Commissioner to China.

Raglan Road was built in 1857, at the conclusion of the Crimean War, and named after Lord Raglan, Commander of the British troops there; he had died in 1855 from dysentery caught in the course of the campaign, during which he had been accused of neglect and incompetence.

On one corner of this junction stands Number 19 Raglan Road, now the Mexican Embassy. The poet Patrick Kavanagh, who lived in this district for many years, resided in the boarding house at this address in 1958 and 1959. Eventually, the house became the headquarters of the

Irish Congress of Trade Unions. One of Kavanagh's most famous poems was 'On Raglan Road', later sung by Luke Kelly of The Dubliners.

On another corner, there is a house owned by Michael O'Leary of Ryanair, while the house on the opposite corner belongs to Denis O'Brien, the telecoms billionaire. One of the most renowned residents of the main terrace of houses in Elgin Road was Delia Murphy, a singer from the west of Ireland, whose husband Tom Kiernan was a high-ranking Irish diplomat before being put in charge of Raidió Éireann (now RTÉ). They lived at 32 Elgin Road from 1935 until 1941, when Kiernan was made Irish Ambassador to the Vatican, an embassy whose closure was announced towards the end of 2011. Waterloo Road and Wellington Road were both laid out and opened up for house building in 1846.

Then: Elgin Road *(Image courtesy of Brian Siggins)*

Inset: Mexican Embassy with Patrick Kavanagh plaque. *(Image by Hugh Oram)*

Now: Junction of Raglan Road and Elgin Road. *(Image by Hugh Oram)*

JUNCTION OF MERRION ROAD AND SANDYMOUNT AVENUE

IN THE OLD photograph, a tram passes on its way to Dalkey; in the modern photograph, a Dublin bus brings the public transport scene on the Merrion Road up to date. However, the setting here wasn't always as green and idyllic. Nearly two centuries ago, after the great harbour at Kingstown, now Dún Laoghaire, had been opened to passenger shipping plying between the port and Holyhead, a pub at this corner did great trade with travellers who had arrived from the latter. The Bird House was a thatched tavern and snack house; if travellers had stepped off the cross-channel packet boat in the evening and were making their way into Dublin city centre, they often spent the night at the Bird House, because it was too dangerous to continue the journey into the centre of Dublin late at night. Robbers often lay in wait for unsuspecting travellers as they went along what is now Merrion Road at the RDS and Northumberland Road.

However, Sandymount Avenue has a more uplifting claim to fame, in the literary world. W.B. Yeats, considered by many to be Ireland's greatest poet (alongside Sandymount resident Seamus Heaney), was born at Number 5 Sandymount Avenue (also known as Number 1 George's Ville) in 1885. When Yeats was a young boy his family moved to London and he didn't return to Ireland until he was fifteen.

A little further down the road, at Number 11 Sandymount Avenue, T.C. Murray (1873-1959), considered one of the greatest of the Abbey Theatre playwrights, lived for many years. A teacher by profession, he was made headmaster of the Inchicore Model Schools in 1915. He only started writing for the theatre in middle age, but went on to write fifteen superbly crafted plays.

A veteran of the media since the early 1960s, Gay Byrne, renowned as the first and longest-serving host of *The Late Late Show* on RTÉ television, lives with his wife Kathleen in a luxury apartment on the site of the old headquarters of Teagasc, the farm research and development organisation, now headquartered in Carlow.

Then: Tram at the corner of Merrion Road and Sandymount Avenue. (*Image courtesy of Pat Herbert*)

Now: Junction of Merrion Road and Sandymount Avenue. (*Image by Hugh Oram*)

AILESBURY ROAD

WHEN AILESBURY ROAD was built towards the end of the nineteenth century, it was the longest road in Ireland, at 1 mile (1.6km). It was named after the Marquis of Ailesbury, connected by marriage to the Earls of Pembroke, who once owned much of the area.

The houses in the photo were built in the 1880s by Joseph Michael Meade, Lord Mayor of Dublin, 1891/2. His firm built numbers 1 to 27 Ailesbury Road and he built a big house for himself at the corner of Ailesbury Road and Merrion Road. He moved in during 1896 and died there in 1900. Later, the house became St Michael's

College; one of its best-known teachers was the late Dermot Morgan who went on to win television fame as Fr Ted.

Then: Aylesbury Road, now Ailesbury Road. (*Image courtesy of Brian Siggins*)

Now: Ailesbury Road. (*Image by Hugh Oram*)

THE FRENCH EMBASSY

THE BIGGEST HOUSE on Ailesbury Road is Number 53, the French Embassy residence. An extraordinary story lies behind its construction.

Around 1849, a homeless, penniless boy called George Bustard, was selling newspapers at Donnybrook Fair when he discovered a notebook filled with cash. He went to great trouble to find the owner, who gave the fourteen-year-old lad a large reward. Bustard used this to buy a one-way ticket to Australia, where he made a fortune as a builder.

He drew up plans for an enormous forty-room house on the nearest site he could get close to Donnybrook Fair. Bustard never lived to see the house built. Instead, it was constructed around 1910 by his son and his three daughters. The last of the daughters, Kate, stayed in the house until the late 1920s; she was a kindly soul who allowed local children to wander through the house and the vast garden. After her death, it was bought by the French government as the residence of the French diplomatic representative to Ireland. This was the start of Ailesbury Road becoming part of Dublin's diplomatic belt. The house has remained the home of successive French ambassadors, although the French unsuccessfully tried to sell the house in 2008 for €60 million.

Directly across the road is a 1920s house that now houses the French Embassy chancellery. Nell Humphreys, who came from a strongly republican family, built it for £8,000 and it was considered the last house built in Ireland with a secret room, which was never discovered by British forces. It was sold to the French government in 1968; they tried, again, unsuccessfully, to sell in in 2008 for €20 million.

Number 46, near the Donnybrook end of the road, was home to the Scottish veterinary surgeon, John Boyd Dunlop, who patented the world's first pneumatic tyre in 1888 and soon afterwards opened the world's first tyre factory, at Upper Stephen Street, off South Great George's Street, Dublin. Another prominent person connected with Ailesbury Road was Edith Colwill, a leading figure in the Irish suffragette movement in the early twentieth century.

Then: The fine house in Ailesbury Road that became the French Embassy residence; this was the largest private house in Ballsbridge. *(Image courtesy of the French Embassy)*

Now: French Embassy residence, Ailesbury Road. (*Image by Hugh Oram*)

NORTHUMBERLAND ROAD

NORTHUMBERLAND ROAD HAS remained largely unchanged since the houses here were built around 1880. The road had a strong connection with Nationalist politics in the earlier twentieth century. Tom Kettle, a Nationalist who was professor of National Economics at UCD, lived with his wife, Mary Sheehy, and a servant, Mary Redmond, at Number 23 Northumberland Road. In those days, it was commonplace for better-off families in the district to have at least one live-in servant, more if they could afford their upkeep. On the outbreak of the First World War, Kettle had been in Belgium helping buy guns for the Irish Volunteers, but was so appalled by the German invasion of Belgium that he joined the British Army, only to be later killed in action.

Shortly after the 1916 Easter Rising, the Sherwood Foresters marched along Northumberland Road to the infamous Battle of Mount Street Bridge, where they suffered heavy casualties. Volunteers had been in place at Number 25 Northumberland Road and at Carisbrooke House, at the Pembroke Road end of the street. At both locations the Volunteers were overrun. As

for Carisbrooke House, it was demolished in the late 1960s, and in 1967 the present-day Carrisbrook House, which includes the Israeli Embassy among its tenants, was built. On the opposite corner, at the same time, the vast block of Lansdowne House was built; it houses branches of such organisations as the Revenue Commissioners.

Northumberland Road achieved further notoriety on Bloody Sunday, 21 November 1920, when Michael Collins organised widespread assassinations of British agents. Two young Royal Irish Constabulary cadets, Frank Garniss and Cecil Morris, were killed in the garden of Number 16 Northumberland Road. In retaliation, that same afternoon, British forces carried out the Croke Park massacre.

The most famous address on Northumberland Road was Number 58, which housed the German legation through the years of the Second World War. At the end of the war, the Taoiseach, Éamon de Valera, went to the home of the head of the German legation, Herr Hempel, in Monkstown, to pay his condolences on the death of Adolf Hitler. The house in Northumberland Road later became home to the Spanish Cultural Institute, which is now located in Lincoln Place.

Today, Northumberland Road is still part of 'Embassy Land', with those of the Czech Republic and Italy. A public relations company, in which noted media personality Terry Prone is involved, has its offices in Northumberland Road. At the Mount Street Bridge end of the road, another well-known public relations personality, Don Hall, son of legendary television star Frank Hall, has his offices.

Then: Northumberland Road. *(Image courtesy of Brian Siggins)*

Now: Northumberland Road. *(Image by Hugh Oram)*

PEMBROKE ROAD, OPPOSITE THE US EMBASSY

PEMBROKE ROAD IS L-shaped, beginning at the end of Upper Baggot Street and ending beside the US Embassy. One of the long-time residents of Pembroke Road, close to Upper Baggot Street, was the poet Patrick Kavanagh, who for years had a flat at Number 62. On one memorable occasion, the then Archbishop of Dublin, Dr John Charles McQuaid, stopped his official car and sent his driver in with a bottle of whiskey and other goodies for the poet. However, Kavanagh refused to open the door, as he was otherwise engaged; he was in bed with a lady of the night from the canal side at nearby Baggot Street Bridge.

This part of Pembroke Street once had the best-known restaurant in Ballsbridge, Le Coq Hardi, at the corner of Wellington Road. It was set up in 1977 by John Howard, the first of the celebrity

chefs, and he ran it for a quarter of a century. It was known for being the home from home of former Taoiseach Charles Haughey. After the building was sold nearly a decade ago, it was taken over by a wine company.

Also long gone from this part of Pembroke Road was Dublin Corporation's civil defence office at Number 21; it is now at Wolfe Tone Quay, near the city centre.

The old photograph was taken before the trams stopped running from the city centre to Blackrock and Dalkey. The Dalkey service was the last to close, on 10 July 1949. The tram seen here is passing what is now the Embassy Grill, still Italian-owned and noted in the district for its takeaways and its sit-down café. It opened in 1950. Next door to it is a double ethnic restaurant; the Koishi Japanese restaurant upstairs and the Chandni Indian restaurant downstairs. Also visible in the photograph is what is now a branch of the Ulster Bank, at the corner of Shelbourne Road and Merrion Road. Previously, a branch of the Bank of Ireland stood on the site.

The only other Italian 'chipper' in Ballsbridge was Cafolla's on Mespil Road, which traded there for over fifty years before being sold in 2007, at the height of the property boom, for €2.7 million. It was turned into Beshoff Bros but still serves fish and chips. Close by is the Mespil Hotel, converted from a Department of Labour office block.

Then: Tram passing what is now the Embassy Grill, Ballsbridge. (*Image courtesy of Pat Herbert*)

Now: Embassy Grill and Ulster Bank, Ballsbridge. (*Image by Hugh Oram*)

PEMBROKE GARDENS

PEMBROKE GARDENS IS just off Baggot Lane, which in turn runs parallel to Pembroke Road. This striking development of mostly two-storey houses with mansard roofs, and also some single-storey dwellings, was constructed by Crampton between 1919 and 1931. Yet another aspect of the Pembroke Estate legacy, they were created as a memorial to the 14th Earl of Pembroke.

The red-brick houses, which have black bricks set into their chimneys, were designed by Henry Vaughan Crawfurth Smith, from England, who was the engineer and architect for the Pembroke Estate from 1902 until his death at the end of the Second World War. His only break in this service had been during the First World War, when he served in the Royal Engineers. Before he came to live in Dublin, most of Smith's work experience had been in England, apart from the period from 1889 to 1891, when he worked for the railway company in Paraguay. He had married his wife, Clarissa Maud, in England in 1895, and their son and their daughter were born before the move to Dublin. From 1911 onwards they lived at Ailesbury Park, but at the end of his life he was living at Number 45 Raglan Road.

Today, the two rows, at right angles to one another, are largely as they were when they were built, complete with a large green to the rear of the houses.

Then: Pembroke Gardens. (*Image courtesy of G. & T. Crampton*)

Now: Pembroke Gardens. (*Image by Hugh Oram*)

UPPER BAGGOT STREET

FINDLATER'S SHOP TRADED at Number 30 Upper Baggot Street from 1890 to 1969. The site is now occupied by Tesco. Findlater's shop had been modernised after the Second World War, when the two pillars on the shop front were removed. Identical pillars remain on the Boots shop next door, once a branch of Hayes, Conyngham & Robinson, the chemists.

For many years, the manager in this branch of Findlater's was Jimmy Greene; a previous manager had been notorious for drinking the profits. On one occasion during the winter of 1923, six guards broke the Christmas window and helped themselves to turkeys and hams. The manager was too drunk to do anything about the situation, merely heading up to Baggot Street Bridge at five to six that evening to catch his customary cab home.

Other grocery shops here in the same era as Findlater's were Leverett & Frye, the Monument Creameries and Lipton's – all long gone. Subsequent supermarkets, like Five Star, which arrived in the 1960s, also vanished. After Findlater's closed, Power's supermarkets (then Quinnsworth) opened on the site; the chain was acquired by Tesco in 1997, at about the same time that Boots took over Hayes, Conyngham & Robinson's chemist's shops.

Around a century ago, when some 210 families lived on Upper Baggot Street, many shopkeepers and their families lived over the shop, literally, such as the Wells family who owned the eponymous chemist's shop at 20 Upper Baggot Street, which is now one of the many coffee shops in the district, and the Bergins, who ran a drapery shop at Number 40. This now houses a branch of Paddy Power, the bookmaker.

Then: Findlater's, Upper Baggot Street. (*Image courtesy of Alex Findlater*)

Now: Tesco, Upper Baggot Street, formerly Findlater's. (*Image by Hugh Oram*)

HERBERT ROAD

THE MOUNT HERBERT HOTEL, Herbert Road, opened as such in 1955 and has been run ever since by the Loughran family, the second and third generations of which are now involved in running what is now called, after much investment, the Sandymount Hotel.

The original houses here were built in 1860; one of them was occupied by Sir Henry Robinson, one of the founders of the HCR chain of chemists' shops. In the eighteenth century, a distiller from Scotland called Haig, whose family was well known in the Scottish industry, built a distillery close to the present-day bridge over the River Dodder, between the hotel and the Aviva Stadium. The original rugby stadium had opened, as an athletics track, in 1872. Haig's distillery ran for

the best part of a century, until it closed down around 1850, following numerous skirmishes with Customs and Excise. Bricks and rubble from the derelict distillery were used in the foundations of the Herbert Road houses a decade later.

George and Rosaleen Loughran came from the North; George from Cookstown, County Tyrone, Rosaleeen from Downpatrick, County Down. They came south to improve their livelihoods and George opened a small servicing garage in Lansdowne Lane in 1952. After they opened the hotel, it flourished as a fully fledged hotel, but in 1963, the Loughrans concentrated on doing bed and breakfast. With 100 rooms, it was the largest B&B in Ireland, as well as a temperance hotel. All that has changed now, following investment of around €5 million in recent years by John Loughran, one of George and Rosaleen's children. Once again, it's a full-service hotel, and in January 2011 it was renamed the Sandymount Hotel, to avoid any confusion with the Herbert Park Hotel.

Then: Sandymount Hotel, formerly the Mount Herbert Hotel, hosting a wedding in 1963. *(Image courtesy of the Sandymount Hotel)*

Now: Sandymount Hotel, Herbert Road. *(Image by Hugh Oram)*

PUBS AND RESTAURANTS OF UPPER BAGGOT STREET

SEARSON'S PUB AND its next-door neighbour in Upper Baggot Street, the Langkawi Malaysian restaurant, stand on the site of Baggotrath Castle. The castle had been built in the fourteenth century and in 1649, as a prelude to the Battle of Rathmines between Cromwellian forces and Royalist forces, a major battle took place at what is now the junction of Waterloo Road and Upper Baggot Street/Pembroke Road. The castle fell into ruin in the early eighteenth century

and those ruins were finally demolished when the first houses were built in Upper Baggot Street in the early years of the nineteenth century. Searson's dates back 150 years, while Langkawi is somewhat younger, founded in 1990. Searson's pub was built by William Davy, maternal grandfather of John Holohan, and took its name from a manager called Searson. The pub closed towards the end of 2011, following a dispute over the rent.

Another bar, almost next door, is even more renowned: the Waterloo, which dates back to around 1840. Until 1948, it sold groceries as much as alcohol, but between 1948 and 1965, it was run as a pub by John Murray. Andy Ryan took it over then, running it until 2002, when he retired; he is still one of the great characters of the district. In 2002, the bar was taken over by Frank and Michael Quinn, who also own the Lansdowne Hotel, and the pub has been substantially refitted in recent years. The Quinns' other properties include The 51 Bar in Haddington Road; they are the eleventh owners since the original Fleming family.

Then: Baggotrath Castle. (*Image courtesy of Ballsbridge, Donnybrook & Sandymount Historical Society*)

Now: Searson's pub, Upper Baggot Street, former site of Baggotrath Castle. (*Image by Hugh Oram*)

THE OLD INTERCONTINENTAL HOTEL, BALLSBRIDGE

THE IRISH AND Intercontinental Hotel Company had been set up in 1960 by Aer Rianta, which at that stage was the authority controlling Dublin Airport, the Gresham Hotel and Pan Am (a now defunct American airline). It decided to build hotels in Dublin, Cork and Limerick. The Dublin hotel was built on part of the botanical gardens run by Trinity College; some of the trees from those gardens can still be seen along the edges of the site.

However, by 1972 the Intercontinental Hotel plan was losing so much money that the hotels were sold to Jurys. It closed its old hotel in Dame Street and turned this Ballsbridge hotel into

Jurys. The nearby Berkeley Court Hotel (now the Clyde Court Hotel) was opened on Lansdowne Road in 1974 by P.V. Doyle. Eventually, the two hotel companies merged to form Jurys Doyle Hotels.

Then, in 2007, it was decided to sell the Jurys site for redevelopment and not long after, the Berkeley Court site was added. A developer, Sean Dunne, had ambitious plans which included a thirty-seven-storey tower and nine other tower blocks, but with the recession that started in 2008, and planning difficulties, the scheme never materialised and now seems unlikely. Dunne set up a company called D4 Hotels to run the hotels while he awaited clearance for his planned developments. The luxury Towers Hotel, built next to Jurys, is now closed. The Ballsbridge Hotel also contained a large supermarket, now closed, while another business tenant in the hotel is Gerry Downey, who runs his men's hairdressing salon there. He was born and brought up in Ballsbridge Terrace, close by, so he remains firmly connected to the area. The Downey family home is now Kite's Chinese restaurant.

Directly across from the Ballsbridge Hotel is a long-standing fixture of the area: the kiosk. It dates back to the 1920s, but before it was built, the Pembroke Fire Brigade used the site for storing emergency ladders. For many years, it was known as Moran's kiosk. Then in 1989, Phil Monahan, the developer behind The Square shopping centre in Tallaght, paid £132,000 for the $3.4m^2$ kiosk. At the time, it was a jaw-dropping property transaction that attracted much media attention. In 1996, the kiosk was leased to O'Brien's Sandwich Bars, but by 2011 it was empty and a new tenant was being sought. A coffee kiosk has now opened.

Then: Intercontinental Hotel. (*Image courtesy of G. & T. Crampton*)

Now: Ballsbridge Hotel, formerly Jurys Hotel. (*Image by Hugh Oram*)

THE WEE STORES AND PEMBROKE ROAD

THE WEE STORES were long a fixture in Pembroke Lane, together with the nearby Pasteur Dairy, often called the 'Pasture' Dairy. The building that houses the Wee Stores was originally a coach house at the back of a house on Pembroke Road and was built around 1850. By 1910, car mechanics were starting to move into these lanes and a decade later, horse-drawn carriages had become largely redundant. About 1920, the old coach house was turned into a shop. Through the 1930s, it was run by a Miss Hanley. In 1941, it was taken over by John Harrison, who also had shops at North King Street and near the Four Courts. For many years, the Wee Stores was run by John Harrison, who died in 1987, and by his wife, Mary Catherine, who died in 1991.

During the Emergency period of the Second World War and through the late 1940s, the 1950s and the 1960s, the shop did well. It supplied all kinds of groceries as well as coal and peat briquettes. The man who lived in Number 2 Waterloo Road, now replaced by an apartment block, grew tomatoes in his greenhouse for the Wee Stores. Another big seller was pipe cleaners, used by women for doing their hair, while coming up to Christmas, long red candles were very popular.

In the 1940s and '50s, the lanes in this area were still very rural; Pembroke Lane had a piggery as did Heytesbury Lane, which also had an abattoir and a woman selling butter. Wellington Lane in the 1950s was a magical place in which to grow up, remembers Jack MacGouran, a Dublin public relations specialist.

The area also used to have a strong artistic tradition and two customers of the Wee Shop, but never at the same time, since they were sworn enemies, were authors Brendan Behan and Paddy Kavanagh. Mary Catherine Harrison, who came from Co. Monaghan, often used to speak with Paddy Kavanagh in a Monaghan dialect. Visual artists, too, like the late Richard Kingston, who lived in Heytesbury Lane, also shopped at the Wee Stores. Members of the aristocracy stopped off there, too, including a Lady Nelson and Lord Gormanstown.

The big change in retailing started in the 1960s with the arrival of the first supermarkets in Upper Baggot Street. Another blow was the introduction of turnover tax in the early 1960s, which hit small shops badly. Since the passing of John Harrison and his wife, their son, Anthony, has let the premises to other retailers; the premises were recently occupied by First Editions, an antiquarian bookshop run by a relative of Anthony Harrison.

The old characters also died out. Dan Harrington from West Cork was well-known in the district. A countryman living in Dublin, he was full of stories of country lore. He had once worked in construction in England before returning home. Dan died in 2002, aged ninety-six, his wife, Mary, having predeceased him by a decade. Another long-time resident of the same row of houses in Pembroke Road was Sheila Walsh, who for years wrote a social diary for the old Irish Press newspaper. She now lives in Co. Donegal.

Then: The Wee Stores, Pembroke Lane. (*Image courtesy of Anthony Harrison*)

Now: The site of the Wee Stores, Pembroke Lane today. (*Image courtesy of Ronan Colgan*)

WEIR'S, UPPER BAGGOT STREET

OF ALL THE shops in this street listed in Thom's Directory for 1911, only one was still trading just over a century later, Weir's hardware, ironmongery and gifts store. William Weir had opened as an ironmonger and sanitary engineer, in 1885. After his son, William junior, died in 1956, the shop closed. A year later, it was turned into a Five Star supermarket owned by the Tullamore firm of D.E. Williams, which also produced Irish Mist liqueur and Tullamore Dew whiskey. The supermarket lasted for almost twenty years. In 1976, the Simon Community operated in the premises.

Then in 1977, Weir's reopened, by now owned by Curust Industries. At the start of 2012, the shop had a major makeover. For the nearly two decades that Weir's was closed, the main hardware shop on the street was Ryder's, which eventually became Murphy's newsagents. The shop is now a branch of Donnybrook Fair.

On this side of Upper Baggot Street, beyond the Spar convenience store, and the headquarters of what had been Fás, the training organisation, is Grant's, a photo and printing shop established by Grant Howie nearly thirty years ago.

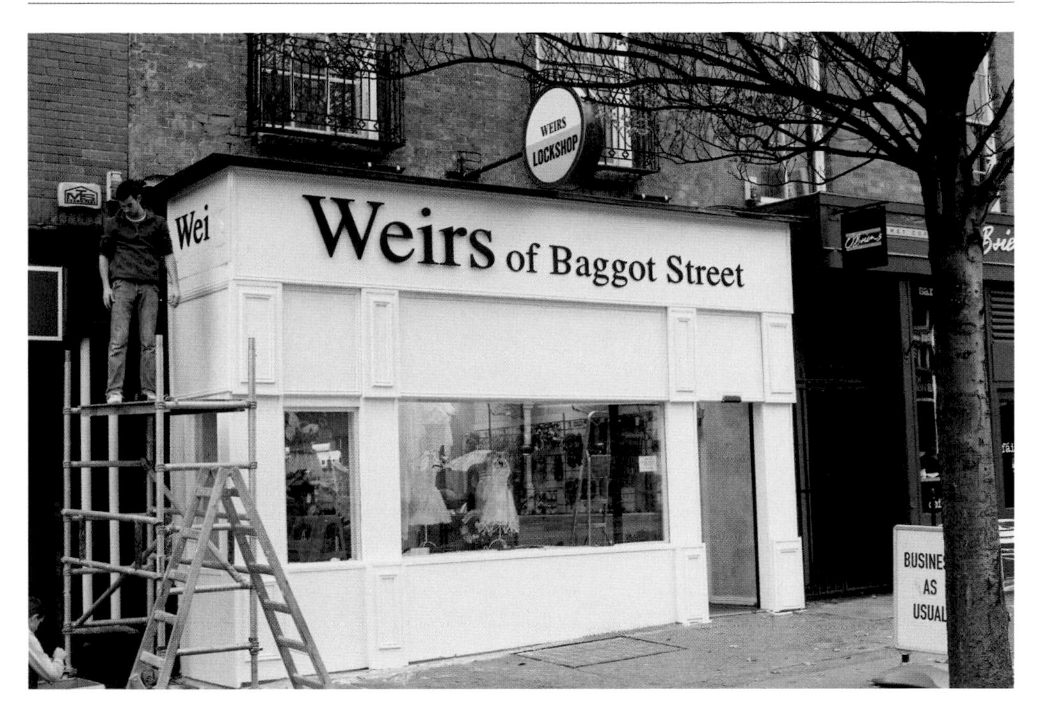

Other notable businesses on this side of the street include Bergin's, the estate agents. The Bergin family are closely connected with the drive by local retailers to turn the street into a heritage quarter. The former Oddbins wine shop, below Bergin's offices, now trades as Baggot Street Wines.

The last of the old style shops on this side of the street was Connell's shoe repair shop, was taken over for an O2 shop, itself now closed.

On the opposite side of the street, Meagher's chemists was opened in 1929 by the Meagher family, who took over a sweet shop. The chemist's is now own by Oonagh O'Hagan.

This side of the street has a Tesco supermarket, which began life in the 1960s as a branch of Power's, in what had been Findlater's. At the far end of this block is a branch of AIB, which before its creation, housed a branch of the Munster & Leinster Bank. In 1961, the branch was completely rebuilt and a brand new idea in banking came to Ireland, the drive- in bank here, which lasted until five years ago.

Many notable places have long since gone, like the Board for the Employment of the Blind, at the corner of Upper Baggot Street and Waterloo Road, where blind people made baskets. The establishment that accommodated 'fallen women' has long since gone and so too has the old Episcopalian church, where St Martin' s House now stands. The old BSA motor bike assembly factory here has long since vanished, as has Wilson's bakery round the corner in Fleming' s Place.

Some restaurants are fondly remembered, like the Horseshoe Café, from the 1960s, close to what is now Tesco and from the 1980s and early 1990s, Kilmartin' s restaurant in what had been Kilmartin' s bookies. The Mercury Travel shop at Number 15 was another victim of changing trends.

Then: Weir's of 21 Upper Baggot Street, 1977. *(Image courtesy of Weir's)*

Now: Weir's of Upper Baggot Street. (*Image by Hugh Oram*)

HAYES, CONYNGHAM & ROBINSON

HAYES, CONYNGHAM & ROBINSON had a chemist's shop in Ballsbridge for many years. The firm had been founded at Number 12 Grafton Street and was incorporated on 8 April 1897. The Ballsbridge shop opened in September that year and like most shops of the time had a delivery boy with a bicycle, who brought prescriptions that had been made up for customers living in the area. For many years, Henry Conyngham, the middle name of the firm, lived at Number 40 Waterloo Road. He died at his residence on 4 April 1931. One of the features of the Ballsbridge shop was the large sign on the side of the building, which simply gave its name; it had been an advertising sign on one of the old Dublin trams.

In April 1988, the chemist's shop closed down and the building was demolished to make way for a new restaurant, Roly's, which opened in 1992. Its partners then were Roly Saul, John O'Sullivan,

Angela O'Sullivan and chef Colin O'Daly. O'Daly said that their aim was to present *haute cuisine* at ready-to-wear prices. Since the restaurant opened, the biggest changes to the premises have been the start of its own bakery on the site, in 1996, and much more recently, the conversion of most of the ground floor to a shop and café. When Roly's opened in 1992, Ballsbridge had 150 restaurant covers (places); by 2006, that figure had jumped to over 1,300.

Next door to Roly's is the Lobster Pot, a traditional silver-service restaurant serving mainly fish dishes that has been open here since 1980. Just around the corner is Kite's Chinese restaurant, at the start of Ballsbridge Terrace; one of the oldest ethnic restaurants in the district. Next door to Roly's is the Bon Espresso newsagent and take-away food shop; a news agency has long featured on this site and for years was known as The Alcove, selling sweets and papers. Just through the narrow archway here is Clyde Lane, where Donald Helme ran an advertising agency for many years. On the far side of the arch is yet another ethnic restaurant, Bella Cuba, started in 1999, which now has a branch in Florida. The next-door pub, Bellamy's, has been known as such since the mid- 1990s, but a pub has existed on this site since 1859.

Ballsbridge Terrace, just round the corner, once had the offices of a Protestant-run Magdalen-style laundry for 'fallen women' at Number 35. The laundry was located next to the Johnston, Mooney & O'Brien bakery in what had been the ruins of Duffy's old calico and cotton mill and at its height, a century ago, had around twenty laundresses.

Then: The Alcove Shop, Ballsbridge. (*Image courtesy of the US Embassy*)

Now: Roly's restaurant, formerly Hayes, Conyngham & Robinson's chemist shop. (*Image by Hugh Oram*)

MERRION ROAD

A CENTURY AGO, this line of shops and houses was described as the north-east side of Merrion Road. On one side of the bridge at Ballsbridge is the entrance to a small network of roads with estate-cottage-style houses. In August 1986, the houses here that face the River Dodder were badly flooded during Hurricane Charlie. On the night of Monday 24 October 2011, a monster rainstorm caused the River Dodder to rise about 6 metres, leading to widespread flooding.

Once, Ballsbridge Cottages faced the river here; a group of a dozen old-fashioned country-style whitewashed cottages known as The Gut, although the origins of this nickname remain obscure.

Just past the entrance road to the present small network of estate-style cottages, starts a line of shops, with two restaurants coming first. Then there's Paddy Byrne's chemist's shop. Before Donal O'Sullivan, a great character in the district, had taken over this pharmacy in 1948, it had once been a greengrocer's shop. It was taken over by John Byrne after Donal O'Sullivan retired in 1973 and has been run by John Byrne's son Paddy since 1991.

Going back to the First World War, a commercial firm, the Standard Accumulator Company, mechanical and electrical engineers, had their offices here and as recently as 1965, a firm called Fryers had similar offices in the same building, Number 6. Next door, at Number 8, was a well-known newsagent and bookseller's called Herbert House, run in the 1960s by Margaret Behan. Number 18, at the end of this terrace, was a rates collection office for Pembroke UDC a century ago. Forty years ago this was home to a Spar shop, which is now halfway along this block. In more recent times, a Sony shop was here and it has now changed use yet again, to a pizza place.

One of the pubs here, Crowe's, has been located on this road for over a century and contains many old photographs of the district. Upstairs, there's now a restaurant called simply 'Roast'. Paddy Cullen's pub and the next-door Mary Mac's are owned by Paddy Cullen, a former Dublin GAA football star. Mary Mac's is the more recent pub, opened in 2000 where Ballsbridge Travel was located. A century ago, the main pub here was the Hibernian Inn. Then, as now, the pubs in Ballsbridge are popular with rugby supporters before and after rugby matches in the nearby Aviva Stadium.

Then: Bridge at Ballsbridge. (*Image courtesy of the Royal Dublin Society library*)

Now: Bridge at Ballsbridge, looking to shops on the Merrion Road. (*Image by Hugh Oram*)

MARIAN COLLEGE

MARIAN COLLEGE, BESIDE the River Dodder and close to the Aviva Stadium, was started by the Marian Fathers in 1954. The school building opened in 1956; originally two storeys, it was expanded to three in 1968. It was built beside Riverside House, whose last occupants were the Lloyd family. The last member of the Lloyd family to live there was Finbarr Lloyd, who died in 1953. Today, the Marist Order has its headquarters in the house.

Among the first pupils at this second-level school were the late Dermot Morgan, the television comic actor, and Noel Pearson, the theatrical and film producer and impresario. The present Catholic Archbishop of Dublin, Diarmuid Martin, was also a student here.

The inset photograph shows Brian Nesbitt, who was the first pupil at the school when it opened. He later returned to the college as a teacher. The pupil with him was Celcis English.

When the college opened its swimming pool in 1966, it was said to have been the first new pool in Dublin in the twentieth century. Today, the school has about 460 second-level students, nearly all male, although since the late 1990s, it has also had about twelve girls a year doing the senior repeat Leaving Certificate course. Pupils come not just from the locality, but from all over Dublin, helped by the school's proximity to the DART station at Lansdowne Road.

On the right-hand side of the old photograph can be seen the old East Stand at Lansdowne Road, for long the headquarters of the Irish Rugby Football Union. The first rugby international was played there on 11 March 1878, when Ireland beat England. The stand seen in here was built in 1927; it was demolished in 1983 and replaced by a much more modern stand. In turn, in 2007 the whole grounds closed for demolition. The new Aviva Stadium, seating 50,000 and regarded as a state-of-the-art arena, opened in 2010, for both rugby and soccer matches. It cost close to €400 million to build.

Marian College has another claim to fame. In the weeks before Telefís Éireann (now RTÉ) went on air for the first time, on the last day of December 1961, much of the training of production personnel was done in the school hall. For a short while after the station started, some programmes were broadcast from the same venue.

Then: Marian College, early 1960s. (*Image courtesy of Marian College*)

Inset: The first student. (Image courtesy of Marian College)

Now: Marian College, Lansdowne Road, with the Aviva Stadium visible to the right. (*Image by Hugh Oram*)

ST BARTHOLOMEW'S CHURCH

ST BARTHOLOMEW'S CHURCH on Clyde Road was consecrated in 1867, at a time when much of Clyde Road was still open fields. Construction of Clyde Road and Clyde Lane had only begun in 1864. The church was designed by an English architect, Thomas Henry Wyatt, and in the original plans he included a spire. This was never built but whether this was due to a shortage of funds or structural instability, no one knows. However, the interior of the church was given very imaginative decorative work, designed by Sir Thomas Deane, who was inspired by Monreale Cathedral in Sicily.

The great vicarage and parish hall next to the church were opened in 1872, but although St Bartholomew's still has the use of the hall, the buildings are now owned by the Knights of Malta.

For long, this Church of Ireland church has been in the High Church tradition. Renowned former curates included George Otto Simms, who eventually became Anglican Archbishop of Armagh and Primate of All-Ireland. The church organ is one of the finest in Dublin and the church has a fine musical heritage; one member of the choir,

Bobby Barden, began singing there in the early 1940s. Regular concerts and other musical presentations are staged in the church. St Bartholomew's is the only place in Ballsbridge where someone can be buried now (but only after cremation), in the new Garden of Remembrance that takes up much of its grounds.

Beneath Clyde Road runs the Swan River, a tributary of the River Dodder, now entirely underground. The Swan comes from the direction of Rathmines and Ranelagh, close to the Royal Hospital in Donnybrook, down Clyde Road and Shelbourne Road, eventually emptying into the Dodder close to Londonbridge Road.

The other Church of Ireland church in Ballsbridge is St Mary's, at the corner of Anglesea Road and Simmonscourt Road, which dates back to 1827. In recent years, a weekly market has been held in its grounds. On the road that bisects Herbert Park can be found a large Edwardian-style house that is home to the First Church of Christ, Scientist.

Then: Clyde Road. (*Image courtesy of Brian Siggins*)

Now: Clyde Road. (*Image by Hugh Oram*)

ST MARY'S CHURCH

ST MARY'S CHURCH and its immediate environs have changed little since this photograph was taken about a century ago. Work on the church began in 1835 and when it was dedicated in 1839, it had neither ceiling nor internal plastering and the floor was earthen. Towards the end of the nineteenth century, the frontage to Haddington Road was extended and the tower was added. The church has fine stained-glass windows.

The parish centre beside the church was opened in 1984. In recent years, the church interior had become very dilapidated but after a major refurbishment of the interior and grounds, the church was reopened at the end of 2011.

St Mary's boys' national school was established in the grounds of the church in 1859 and a new school building was opened in 1939. Most of its pupils start their education at the adjacent St Brigid's primary school. Both schools are thriving, with pupils of many nationalities. St Mary's Holy Faith secondary school for girls nearby on Haddington Road, didn't fare so well; founded in 1904, a new school was built in 1954, but falling numbers and shortage of funds forced it to close in 2007.

One new school in the parish is the International School at the corner of Pembroke Road and Waterloo Road. It replaced the old Pembroke School, known as 'Miss Meredith's'. After she died, it was run for years by the O'Connell sisters. A storm in February 2011, caused a tragic incident here, when an old tree fell on Carolyn Collins, an ESB International worker, as she was walking past, and killed her. She was a daughter of Fergus O' Brien, Lord Mayor of Dublin, 1980/1 and the wife of Richard Collins, financial director of Superquinn.

Another school in the area that continues to expand and thrive is St Conleth's in Clyde Road, which dates back to a house in Clyde Road just before the Second World War.

St Mary's Road, behind Haddington Road church, was built in 1877. What had once been the nurses' home from the old Baggot Street Hospital is now the Dylan Hotel. The pub close to the church on Haddington Road, the 51, owned by the Quinns of the Lansdowne Hotel and Waterloo Bar renown, is one of the oldest in the area, dating back to 1843. It was built with stones from the old Baggotrath Castle.

At the top of Haddington Road, just before the turn into Upper Baggot Street, a number of shops were well established, but even by the end of the 19th century, some had fallen vacant. A new out-patients department for the adjacent hospital was built on this site just over fifty years ago.

Then: St Mary's church, Haddington Road. (*Image courtesy of St Mary's*)

Now: St Mary's church, Haddington Road. (*Image by Hugh Oram*)

THE OLD VETERINARY COLLEGE

THE OLD VETERINARY COLLEGE was opened on Shelbourne Road in 1900, close to the old Hammersmith Works of Crampton the builders, which fronted onto Pembroke Road. The college was extended in 1907/8 and the new buildings were opened by the then Chief Secretary, Augustine Birrell, on 16 January 1909. The college was taken over in 1914 by the Department of Agriculture, not becoming the faculty for Veterinary Science in UCD until 1946. However, the department remained involved until 1960, when the two veterinary schools, one for UCD, the other for Trinity College, were set up at Ballsbridge. They were merged in 1977.

By 2002, the college had moved to state-of-the-art facilities on UCD's Belfield campus. The site at Shelbourne Road was subsequently sold for redevelopment, making over €170 million, but plans to build a nine-storey office block on the site were turned down in 2009, and in 2012,

the site is still an overflow storage car park for Ballsbridge Motors, across the road. The actual site is now said to be worth around €20 million.

Then: Veterinary College. (*Images courtesy of G. & T. Crampton*)

Now: Site of the old Veterinary College, Shelbourne Road. (*Image by Hugh Oram*)

THE OLD PEMBROKE TOWN HALL

THIS PHOTOGRAPH SHOWS the old town hall of the Pembroke Township, which was absorbed into Dublin Corporation in 1930. The township was set up in 1863 and they wasted comparatively little time in getting a grandiose town hall built. In March 1879, a local builder, a Mr Graham, successfully tendered for building the town hall, the construction of which was partially funded with a loan from the Bank of Ireland. The Pembroke Estate gave the site free of charge; it had been part of a field that stretched to Simmonscourt Road. The Pembroke Estate also paid two thirds of the cost of the new building.

The building was designed in an elaborate neo-Gothic style, complete with a magnificent stained-glass window at the top of the main stairway. It was noted that so many senior civil servants and army officers lived in the district that disproportionate attention was given by the people in the town hall to sanitary matters.

With the new town hall, the township was also able to improve its fire-fighting facilities, since the building incorporated a small fire station. In the 1860s, if a fire occurred in the township, firemen and horse-drawn equipment were sent out, but the owner or occupier of any building that caught fire had to pay half the cost of putting out the blaze. By 1892, the fire brigade in the town hall consisted of a supervisor and four men.

In the immediate aftermath of the 1916 Easter Rising, Éamon de Valera, who had been in charge of the rebels at Boland's Mill, was held captive in the weights and measures office in Pembroke Town Hall. At the corner of Herbert Park and Elgin Road stands an Old IRA monument, which was dedicated by de Valera in 1973, in his last public engagement before retiring from the Presidency of Ireland.

The Pembroke Township, however, was relatively short-lived; it was abolished in 1930 and Pembroke, including Ballsbridge, became part of Dublin Corporation. The old town hall was taken over by Ringsend Technical School, which stayed there until 1951. The Dublin Vocational Education Committee then moved in and the building has been its headquarters ever since.

Then: Pembroke Town Hall. (*Image courtesy of Brian Siggins*)

Inset: Army personnel at the Pembroke Town Hall during the Second World War. (*Image courtesy of Brian Siggins*)

Now: Old fire station at the former Pembroke Town Hall. (*Image by Hugh Oram*)

THE PEMBROKE LIBRARY

THE PEMBROKE LIBRARY in Anglesea Road opened in 1929. It was one of eighty libraries built throughout Ireland with grants from the Carnegie Trust, founded by Andrew Carnegie, a Scottish-American billionaire and philanthropist. In 1912, the plan had been to build two Carnegie libraries in the Pembroke Township – one in Ballsbridge, the other in Ringsend – but in 1925, the Pembroke Council decided to go ahead with just one, the library in Ballsbridge. It was built at a cost of around £7,000 on a site adjacent to the Pembroke Town Hall. The architect was W.H. Hendy of Kaye Parry Ross & Hendy, and one of the quantity surveyors on the project was W.F. Beckett, father of Samuel Beckett.

The formal opening of the library took place on 29 September 1929. The first librarian was Frank O'Connor, whose real name was Michael O'Donovan. While he worked there, he lived in a

flat further along Anglesea Road. Born in Cork in 1903 and brought up in poverty, his formal education had ended at the age of twelve. As an anti-Treaty combatant, he was interned by the new Irish Free State Government at Gormanstown, County Meath, in 1922/3. His job at the Pembroke Library gave O'Connor a way into Dublin literary circles, where he soon proved a disruptive influence. Within two years of starting his library job, one of his best-known books was published: a collection of short stories entitled *Guests of the Nation* (1931). A bust of O'Connor was subsequently erected in the library.

The Pembroke Library has long since been part of the Dublin City Council's library service and extensive improvements to the interior of the building were completed in August 2010. The facade remains unchanged since it was built over eighty years ago. The Ballsbridge, Donnybrook and Sandymount Historical Society, whose chairman is John Holohan, is based at the library.

Then: Anglesea Road Library. (*Image courtesy of G. & T. Crampton*)

Now: Anglesea Road Library today. (*Image by Hugh Oram*)

MERRION ROAD RAILWAY STATION

MERRION ROAD ONCE had a railway station, beside where the Horse Show House pub now stands, directly opposite the RDS. In 1893, a branch siding had been opened from the main Westland Row to Kingstown line, passing through Ballsbridge, and for a short time afterwards maintenance work on railway engines was done here. By 1899, a railway station had opened at the end of this branch line, but it was only used while shows were being staged at the RDS.

The branch line was also used for bringing horses to RDS shows. That system was in place until 1971, before the start of construction of the AIB headquarters on the site of the old RDS sale paddock and its accompanying cottages.

As for the main railway line through Ballsbridge, it had opened in 1834 as the world's first commuter railway line. The gates on the line at Lansdowne Road were built at the same time. However, the railway station at Lansdowne Road, which initially included Ballsbridge in its title, didn't open until 1 July 1870.

Within a short time of the new railway opening, a great flood on 7 November 1834 swept away the first railway bridge over the River Dodder, while debris that swept down the river from Rathfarnham and Rathgar also destroyed the new bridge at Ball's Bridge. However, within three weeks of the flood, a new timber bridge was in place to replace the wrecked railway bridge. This was replaced in 1847 by another timber bridge. Another, built in 1851, survived until 1934, when the bridge was completely rebuilt.

The main road bridge across the River Dodder at Ballsbridge was first built in 1791, but after the 1834 flood it was replaced with a stone bridge, which opened in 1835. This bridge was substantially widened and improved in 1904 and it is this bridge that still stands today.

Then: Locomotive at old RDS siding. (*Image courtesy of the Royal Dublin Society library*)

Now: Horse Show House pub, beside the site of the former RDS railway siding and station. *(Image by Hugh Oram)*

BAGGOT STREET HOSPITAL

THIS PHOTOGRAPH SHOWS the original incarnation of Baggot Street Hospital, built in 1832 as a fifty-two-bed hospital. Alterations were made in 1837 and 1851, then in 1892 the hospital was rebuilt. Its characteristic facade, constructed from red brick and terracotta, makes it a very striking building on Upper Baggot Street to this day. At Eastmoreland Place nearby, a nurses' home was built in a similar style in 1900; it was sold in 1988 for conversion to apartments but became a hotel, and today the building is occupied by the ultra-trendy Dylan Hotel. As for the hospital itself, it was a voluntary institution for 150 years, but in 1988 its board ceded the use of the hospital to what

was then the Eastern Health Board. Today, it is run by the HSE as a community hospital. Many characters were long associated with the hospital, including Alice the flower seller, who, around fifty years ago, had a pitch outside the front entrance, and Dr Carthage Carroll, a noted medical man who was closely connected with the hospital at around the same time.

Then: Old Baggot Street Hospital. (*Image courtesy of G.A. Duncan*)

Now: The site of Baggot Street Hospital today. *(Image by Hugh Oram)*

HERBERT PARK

THIS POND IS all that is left of the great International Exhibition staged in 1907 on land given by the Pembroke Estate, which four years later, in 1911, was reincarnated as Herbert Park, which covers 32 acres (13 hectares). The main entrance to the great exhibition was close to the present-day Roly's restaurant and the Ballsbridge end of the road that runs through Herbert Park. Another way into the great exhibition was through the Morehampton Road entrance. The exhibition had an enormous array of displays, from all corners of the then British Empire and beyond: everything from a traditional

Irish thatched cottage to elaborate pavilions representing countries around the world, such as France and Canada. Altogether, close to three million people visited the exhibition.

One of its star attractions was the Canadian water chute. It cost £3,241 to build and its takings during the show were more than double that, such was its popularity. Visitors who climbed to the top of the chute had a spectacular view over the whole layout of the exhibition. They then climbed into small wagons that ran on two parallel tracks down into the lake. The wagons were then retrieved from the water and hauled back to the top of the chute, ready for another load of thrill-seeking visitors.

The water chute was dismantled after the exhibition closed, but the lake remains to this day as the Herbert Park duck pond.

Herbert Park was officially opened on 19 August 1911; the Earl of Pembroke had given the land to Pembroke UDC for the people of the district, to commemorate the coming of age of his son Lord Herbert, after whom the park is named.

Then: Herbert Park bandstand. (*Image courtesy of Brian Siggins*)

Now: Herbert Park bandstand today. (*Image by Hugh Oram*)

DUCK POND IN HERBERT PARK

THE YEAR AFTER the great exhibition closed, the Dublin Society of Model and Experimental Engineers started sailing model boats on the pond. It also built a miniature steam railway on a 32-metre-long elevated track in what is now the tennis-courts side of the park, but in 1978, moved the railway to Marlay Park in Rathfarnham, which doesn't have a pond. Now, the Irish Model Boat Club sails model boats on the duck pond every Saturday afternoon, all year, and on Wednesday evenings in summer.

Ireland's first municipal bowls green was opened in the park in 1944. The Herbert Park Croquet Club came into existence in 1986. It has around forty members, using two lawns. More recent innovations in the park have included a children's playground and, since 2011, allotments.

Then: Herbert Park duck pond. (*Image courtesy of Brian Siggins*)

Now: The duck pond in Herbert Park today. (*Image by Hugh Oram*)

BEGGAR'S BUSH BARRACKS

BEGGAR'S BUSH BARRACKS were built in 1827 and their eastern side ran as far as the western bank of the River Dodder, which is now Shelbourne Road. The barracks were used as a training depot for the British garrison in Ireland and the old photograph, taken in October 1868, shows soldiers in bearskin caps, who were members of the 3rd Battalion Grenadiers. After the Anglo-Irish Treaty, the barracks were the first to be handed over by the British to the provisional government, represented by Michael Collins, on 31 January 1922. Just over two years later, on 22 November 1924, Robert Erskine Childers, who was a Republican opposed to the Treaty, was executed at the barracks. He was the father of Erskine Childers, who was President of Ireland

for a brief period in 1973/4, before he collapsed and died from a heart attack after less than two years in office.

The barracks were closed down later in the 1920s and these days, the great open square, together with the former quarters for cavalry and infantry, have been sympathetically refurbished. Many new buildings have also been added. A number of public offices are located there, including the Labour Relations Commission and the Geological Survey, while the Irish Labour History Society has a museum there. New apartments provide luxurious living quarters for many, while part of the old quarters have been converted into sheltered housing for older people.

A print museum had been opened in the basement of the Irish Print Union in Lower Gardiner Street in central Dublin in 1990, but it soon proved too small. Fortuitously, the old garrison chapel at Beggar's Bush became available and it was converted into the National Print Museum, which was formally opened by the then President, Mary Robinson, in 1996. In 2011, the museum underwent a substantial refurbishment. As for the original name of Beggar's Bush, it relates to a large bush that stood on the site until the barracks were built. Many local beggars used to take shelter under the bush until they ventured out to look for money-making opportunities in the city centre. This area was also noted for its highwaymen and in the early nineteenth century, newspapers reported numerous robberies in this area.

Then: Soldiers at Beggar's Bush Barracks. (*Image courtesy of the National Print Museum/Irish Architectural Archives*)

Inset: Victorian Soldiers at Beggar's Bush Barracks. (*Image courtesy of the National Print Museum/Irish Architectural Archives*)

Now: Sheltered housing for older people at Beggar's Bush *(Image by Hugh Oram)*

THE CHESTER BEATTY LIBRARY

THE CHESTER BEATTY LIBRARY used to be in Shrewsbury Road; it moved to the Clock Tower building in Dublin Castle in 2000. Despite plans to redevelop the Shrewsbury Road site for luxury housing, it remains derelict and boarded up.

Sir Alfred Chester Beatty was an American mining magnate, who developed a remarkable collection of Asian art. In 1950, he moved his collection from Britain to Dublin, for tax reasons, and his home to Ailesbury Road.

He became an honorary Irish citizen in 1957; after he died in Monte Carlo in 1968, he became the first Irish citizen to get a State funeral. The original building for the Chester Beatty Library was built in 1951/2 and extended in 1954. The construction work included a house for the librarian. The library was opened to researchers in 1953, then later to the general public. A new gallery was opened in 1973, but before long it became clear that the library would have to move to a bigger site.

Other houses on Shrewsbury Road have been put up for sale in recent years. A house called Walford was sold in 2005 for €58 million, but by 2011 was advertised for sale again, for a mere €15 million. Another big house that was up for sale in 2011 was the headquarters of the Pharmaceutical Society of Ireland. This extraordinarily lavish house was once owned by John C. Parkes, owner of a brass and iron foundry in the Coombe. During the flamboyant years of the Celtic Tiger, many Irish millionaires bought property in Shrewsbury Road, but their numbers have now dwindled, so much so that the *Sunday Independent* said 'millionaires' road' now shows signs of the dreaded ghost-estate syndrome.

Then: Chester Beatty Library, shortly after it was constructed at Shrewsbury Road, 1950s. (*Image courtesy of the Trustees of the Chester Beatty Library, Dublin*)

Now: Entrance to the old Chester Beatty Library, Shrewsbury Road. (*Image by Hugh Oram*)

SIMMONSCOURT BUILDING, RDS

THIS DOWDY BUILDING was originally constructed to provide accommodation for stable hands and other workers who had come from the country to attend the various shows at the RDS, especially the Horse Show. The accommodation was rudimentary; they slept four to a room and the washrooms were communal. After the Troubles began in Derry in 1969, then Belfast in 1970, many people fled Nationalist areas of Belfast especially and for a while, refugees from the

North were housed in this block. Recently, the building housed the offices for the 2012 Eucharistic Congress, which was staged mainly in the RDS.

The area close to the Simmonscourt Building has been much developed in recent years. Beside it, the Four Seasons Hotel was opened at the start of the first decade of the new millennium. Shortly after it opened, Robert O'Byrne wrote a devastating critique of its architectural style in *The Irish Times* – an article that caused great controversy at the time. One of the residents of the luxury apartments within the hotel is former Taoiseach Albert Reynolds and his wife Kathleen.

On the opposite corner of Simmonscourt Road is another hotel, Bewley's, converted from what had been the Masonic Girls' School. Right across Simmonscourt Road from the Simmonscourt Building are two substantial office blocks. Eventually, the RDS plans to redevelop the site of the Simmonscourt Building. Also on Simmonscourt Road is the convent of the Poor Clares, which dates back to 1905.

Then: Simmonscourt Building, RDS. (*Image courtesy of the Royal Dublin Society library*)

Now: Simmonscourt Building, RDS today. (*Image by Hugh Oram*)

SHELBOURNE ROAD POST OFFICE

Ballsbridge District Office (built c. 1890)

BUILT IN 1890, the post office was one of the first commercial buildings on Shelbourne Road. Extensive modifications were made in 1913-15. The post office remains open today, the original red-brick facade untouched. Next door is the Ballsbridge College of Further Education. Originally, the Pembroke Technical School was established here in 1903. The present building was constructed in 1950; before that, part of the site was occupied by a large corrugated-iron hut, used for teaching domestic subjects for women, such as laundry and cooking.

At the time that the post office was built, Shelbourne Road had a mere handful of shops and commercial premises. Most of the houses directly across from the post office were tenements. These days, there is a good selection of restaurants, including Maia and the Jewel in the Crown, an Indian restaurant. The French Paradox wine shop and wine bar was opened a decade ago.

That building had been one of the traditional two-up, two-down houses common in the area until Dr Anne Legge, a GP, converted it into her surgery. She was killed in a car crash outside the old Jurys Hotel in 1987. For five years, the premises, which stayed in the family, remained unused, but were then converted into the French Paradox. Also on that side of Shelbourne Road is Trim, a women's hairdresser's, which used to trade as Dee Bees, nearby on the main Merrion Road, near the bridge.

Turner's Cottages was an enclave of tenement buildings off this side of the Shelbourne Road. About twenty-six houses offered extremely basic accommodation; children played in their bare feet in the secluded street. Turner's Cottages were named after Richard Turner, who set up his Hammersmith Ironworks close by in the mid-1830s. The cottages, built to house some of Turner's workers, managed to last until the early 1970s, when they were demolished and replaced by a mundane office block that still stands on the site.

On the other side of Shelbourne Road, between the college and the traffic lights at the junction with Merrion Road, was a branch of the old First National Building Society. Carmel Skehan, who was the sister of the society's long-time managing director, John Skehan, had a 'grace and favour' apartment above the branch. She died in 1999. Since then, the whole premises has been extensively remodelled and now houses a branch of Sherry FitzGerald, the estate agents.

Until the 1860s, Shelbourne Road had been known as Artichoke Road, after a French Huguenot, John Villiboise, acquired land close to the present-day Holles Street, where he cultivated artichokes. What became Artichoke Road ran all the way from there to the top of the present-day Shelbourne Road.

Then: A postcard depicting Shelbourne Road post office. (*Image courtesy of the Royal Dublin Society library*)

Now: Shelbourne Road post office today. (*Image by Hugh Oram*)

THE RDS CLOCK TOWER

THIS OLD PHOTOGRAPH shows the clock tower of the Royal Dublin Society as it was in 1953. The RDS is one of Ireland's venerable institutions, and has long been a key organisation in Ballsbridge, but it wasn't always that way. It was established in Dublin in 1731 with the aim of promoting husbandry (agriculture) and industry. Within a fortnight of its foundation, science was added to its title. It didn't become the Royal Dublin Society until King George IV conferred the title in 1820. It had been granted its charter on 2 April 1750.

During the eighteenth century, it operated at various addresses in the city centre, including Marlborough Street and Poolbeg Street, before buying Leinster House in Kildare Street from the FitzGerald family in the early nineteenth century, for £20,000.

During the nineteenth century, the society created many advances, ranging from the botanic gardens at Glasnevin to a school of art and design, and laying the foundations for the National Museum and the National Library. The development of the Spring Show began in 1830, while from the mid-1860s, the society held its Horse Show on the lawns of Leinster House.

The move to Ballsbridge began in earnest in 1871, when the society held a show in a field there for the first time. In 1879, the Earl of Pembroke granted a lease to the society of 15 acres of land (6 hectares) at Ballsbridge, fronting onto what was then Ball's Bridge Road (now Merrion Road). The society had its new premises ready for the Spring Show in 1881. Today, the facilities have been expanded enormously, with a range of halls that are used for many exhibitions and conferences. The arena has been developed for sports and other uses, including outdoor musical events, and is home to the Leinster rugby team.

On the far side of Simmonscourt Road, the

Simmonscourt Pavilion is a vast arena that can hold up to 7,000 people, which has been used, on occasion, for staging the Eurovision Song Contest. Two large office blocks were built close to this pavilion but the biggest development on the main site in recent years has been the construction of the Four Seasons Hotel.

Other-present day facilities on the main RDS site include the Concert Hall, the new library, which was opened in 1965, and the bar and lounge for members.

When the Irish Free State came into being in 1922, the RDS began to hand over Leinster House to the new government. At the request of Michael Collins, the main assembly room was handed over, and in August 1924 the whole of Leinster House was taken over as temporary accommodation for the Houses of the Oireachtas, which are still in situ.

Then: Clock Tower, RDS, on front cover of *Ireland of the Welcomes*, 1953. (*Image courtesy of the Royal Dublin Society library*)

Inset: Visitors arriving at the RDS. (*Image courtesy of the Royal Dublin Society library*)

Now: Clock Tower, RDS. (*Image by Hugh Oram*)

THE RDS MAIN HALL

DIRECTLY ACROSS FROM the Main Hall of the RDS is a cul de sac called Sydenham Road. It was here that Joseph Hepburn-Ruston, father of film star Audrey Hepburn, lived at the end of his life. During the Second World War, he had been interned on the Isle of Man for his fascist views, but after the war he settled in Dublin. One of the last times that he met his famous daughter was in 1964, when Audrey came to Dublin for the Irish premiere of *My Fair Lady*. In the last years of his life, her father was a familiar figure walking around Ballsbridge.

Another anecdote from this immediate area also concerns the RDS. Bridie McManus from County Kerry used to live in Ballsbridge Avenue, just opposite the main hall of the RDS. In earlier days, when the Spring Show and Horse Show were in full swing, as many as fifty or sixty Gardaí were on point duty here. Many were from the country and it's said that Bridie Mac had a soft spot for any countrymen who found themselves in Dublin, especially if they were in uniform. It became a long tradition that once Gardaí had gone off duty at the RDS, they would retire to Bridie's house for tea and her renowned apple tarts.

Then: Main Hall at RDS, *c*. 1920. (*Image courtesy of the Royal Dublin Society library*)

Inset: Residential cottages opposite the RDS. (*Image courtesy of the Royal Dublin Society library*)

Now: Main Hall, RDS today. (*Image by Hugh Oram*)

THE RDS SALE PADDOCK

THE RDS SALE PADDOCK was a 6.5 hectare site used for horse sales for many years. After the First World War, sales dropped so much that they were worth a mere £22,000 a year. In 1922, the sales were taken over by Goffs. By 1946, just after the end of the Second World War, sales had risen significantly, to around £500,000 a year, attracting many buyers from Britain, the continent and

further afield. No fewer than eight winners of the Grand National had been bought here. The whole site of the sale paddock was sold to AIB in the early 1970s, so that it could construct its new bank centre there. The original centre, with 4,000m2 of office space, was one of the first new-style business campuses in Ireland. Recently, the large pond at the front of the original centre was filled in and the entire area was paved over. In the past few years, much extra office space has been added at the rear of the original complex.

Beside the sale paddock were some cottages, Ballsbridge Cottages, which, by the start of the twentieth century, had turned into slum dwellings, where families lived in extreme poverty. Many of the houses had fallen into ruin by the time of the First World War.

Then: Cottages beside the old RDS sales paddock, now site of AIB Bankcentre. (*Image courtesy of the Royal Dublin Society library*)

Inset: Aerial view of Ballsbridge. (*Image courtesy of the Royal Dublin Society library*)

Now: The headquarters of AIB. (*Image by Hugh Oram*)

THE SPRING SHOW

THIS DELIGHTFUL PHOTOGRAPH, taken around 1912, shows horse-drawn laundry vans going in procession to the RDS Spring Show. On the left-hand side of the photograph can be seen the old Carisbrooke House, while in the middle distance in the centre of the photograph is a tram on the route from Nelson's Pillar in what is now O'Connell Street, headed towards Dalkey. The railings on the right-hand side of the photograph fence in the old Trinity College botanical gardens. Subsequently, in the early 1960s, a hotel was built here, which eventually became Jury's Hotel.

The Court Laundry had its headquarters at the corner of Hatch Street and Harcourt Street; the headquarters of the old Agricultural Credit Corporation were subsequently built on the site. The four-year-old laundry had been bought as a going concern by H.C. Watson from its founder, a Mr Finney, in 1907. Watson introduced many improvements and eventually, in 1961, sold it to his cousin, A.B. Goodbody from Galway. The laundry closed in 1971.

Its primrose yellow vans delivered laundry all over Dublin and even as far as Balbriggan and Skerries. For younger workers, going to the Spring Show was a gala event, although no women were allowed to go to the RDS aboard one of these vans.

The laundry vans assembled at St Stephen's Green and made their way in procession via Pembroke Road to the RDS. Horse-drawn vans at the Spring Show started to decline in the 1930s, while the Spring Show itself vanished from the scene in the 1990s.

The Spring Show of 1923 saw an innovation in broadcasting, when the Marconi Company operated a live radio operation for three days – the first time that the

new-fangled wireless had been heard in public. Transmissions to the stand came from the Royal Marine Hotel in what was then Kingstown, now Dún Laoghaire.

Years later, the RDS also hosted the first public demonstration of television in this part of Ireland, at the Spring Show in 1951. The company involved was Pye (Ireland), which was based in Dundrum

Then: Court Laundry, a procession of horse drawn laundry vans going through Ballsbridge to the RDS spring show, c. 1912. *(Courtesy of Robert Tweedy)*

Inset: Marconi stand at RDS, 1923. (*Image courtesy of the Royal Dublin Society library*)

Now: Carrisbrook House (on the left) with Pembroke Road in the foreground *(Image by Hugh Oram)*

GUINNESS SUMMER FETES AT THE RDS

IN THE EARLY part of the twentieth century, workers from the Guinness brewery and their families attended summer fetes at the RDS, which were organised for them by the company. These events included races and other sporting fixtures, while vast amounts of food and refreshments were consumed by the many visitors. After the 1909 Guinness fete at the RDS, *The Leader* newspaper reported that men 'were allowed to get beastly drunk, on drink supplied, on what was, for the time being, Guinness's premises'. The fete the previous year (1908) conjured up even more lurid prose, as the paper referred to the scenes of blood, brutality and drunkenness associated with the Guinness sports at Ballsbridge.

Then: Race at Guinness sports day. (*Image courtesy of Guinness Archives*)

Inset: Tug o'war at Guinness sports day. (*Image courtesy of Guinness Archives*)

Now: The present-day rugby stadium, due for some redevelopment. *(Image by Hugh Oram)*

MOTOR SHOW AT THE RDS

PUBLIC ACCEPTANCE OF the new-fangled motor car was quick in Ireland. The first Ford Model N cars went on sale in Ireland in 1907 and by 1913, 600 Fords were registered in Ireland, representing 10 per cent of total car sales.

The Irish Automobile Club staged its first motor show, in what is now the main hall at the RDS in 1907 and this photograph shows the second such show, staged by the club the following year. The show held in January 1908, and seen here, was very successful and includes marques that are still well recognised today, such as Cadillac and Rover, as well as other marques that have long since disappeared, such as Argyll, Berliet, Humber and Sunbeam.

Then: First motor show at the RDS, 1908. *(Image courtesy of Bob Montgomery)*

Inset: Cars parked at the RDS horse show, 1909. *(Image courtesy of Bob Montgomery)*

Now: An unusual sight, an empty Main Hall in the RDS, which is usually busy throughout the year with a constant variety of exhibitions, conferences and other events. The car show was staged here in 1908. *(Image by Hugh Oram)*

THE OLD TRINITY COLLEGE BOTANICAL GARDENS, LANSDOWNE ROAD

TRINITY COLLEGE HAD opened its Physic Garden in the grounds of the college, but by the 1760s, the garden had been moved to Harold's Cross. In July 1806, the college took a 175-year lease, at 15 guineas a year, on 1.2 hectares of land on Shelbourne Road. Subsequently, 0.8 hectares of land was taken off Pembroke Road, then in 1848, 0.8 hectares was leased adjacent to Lansdowne Road. The total area of the garden was just over 3 hectares.

The gardens were renowned for their many rare species of plants, flowers and trees from all over the world, and were visited by many international botanists. The site wasn't particularly interesting because it was flat, but it did have some ponds to break the monotony. By the mid-nineteenth century, the garden was suffering from the effects of the nearby main roads, which weren't covered in tarmac and produced much dust. Smoke from the chimneys of nearby houses was also a problem, as were fumes from the adjacent ironworks of Richard Turner.

In 1942, Trinity College gave part of the land to the next-door Veterinary College, which was expanding. In the early 1960s, the Intercontinental Hotel was built on part of the grounds, while the Berkeley Court Hotel was built on what was left, in the early 1970s.

Trees from the old gardens can still be seen adjacent to Lansdowne Road and Pembroke Road, while close to the entrance to the Ballsbridge Hotel is a giant Californian Redwood tree, the largest relic of the gardens.

Then: Trinity College Botanic Gardens at Lansdowne Road/Pembroke Road/Shelbourne Road. (*Image courtesy of OPW/National Botanic Gardens*)

Now: Californian Redwood in the grounds of the Ballsbridge Hotel. (*Image by Hugh Oram*)

THE US EMBASSY, BALLSBRIDGE

ONE OF ONLY three purpose-built embassies in Dublin (the others are the British and the German embassies), the new US Embassy was opened in May 1964. Previously, the American diplomatic mission had been in Merrion Square. When the design for the new Embassy, by Connecticut-based architect John MacL. Johansen, was unveiled in 1957, there was uproar in Dublin. It was unfavourably received, yet by 1969 An Taisce had given the Embassy its premier award. In the past year or two, there has been much concern that the Embassy might leave Ballsbridge for larger premises elsewhere in the city.

The design was certainly striking. The five-storey building had a circular design and construction by Crampton began in 1962, using as much Irish material as possible. The new Embassy was built on the site of Lea House, which fronted onto both Pembroke Road and Elgin Road. It housed the Irish Tourist Association and then, after it began in 1952, Bord Fáilte. It also housed the offices of a company specialising in radio advertising.

The construction of the US Embassy opened the floodgates for the subsequent rash of new office buildings in Ballsbridge. Between 1964 and 1966, Sisk built the twelve-storey Ardoyne House, a luxury apartment development off Pembroke Park, overlooking Herbert Park.

Then: US Embassy. (*Image courtesy of the US Embassy*)
Inset: US Embassy under construction, 1962-4. (*Image courtesy of the US Embassy*)
Now: US Embassy. (*Image by Hugh Oram*)

VOLUNTEER CREW, OLD PEMBROKE TOWN HALL FIRE STATION

THE LOCAL SECURITY FORCE had been set up in June 1940, soon after the start of the Second World War 'Emergency', and within three months had grown to 180,000 men. Then in January 1941, the combat group of this volunteer force was hived off to form the Local Defence Forces. Just across from the town hall, where Anglesea Road feeds into the main Merrion Road, one building was put up in 1943, at the height of the war-time scarcities: a public toilet block. These toilets have

long been derelict, but Dublin City Council is seeking an alterative use for them. One idea that has been put forward is to turn it into a local museum.

The military theme continued in Ballsbridge for some years after the end of the Second World War, when spectacular military tattoos were staged in the grounds of the RDS.

Then: Pembroke Fire Station. (*Image courtesy of G. & T. Crampton*)

Inset: Pembroke Fire Station, 1902.

Now: Old Pembroke Town Hall, Ballsbridge, now headquarters of the City of Dublin Vocational Education Committee. (*Image by Hugh Oram*)

SWASTIKA LAUNDRY

THE SWASTIKA LAUNDRY on Shelbourne Road dates back to 1912. It was founded by one of the pioneers of the laundry business in Dublin, John W. Brittain, who came from County Leitrim. He had founded the Metropolitan and the White Heather Laundries in Dublin in 1899. When he set up his laundry in Shelbourne Road, he adopted the swastika as its logo; the swastika was originally an ancient symbol of good luck in India and the Sanskrit word had entirely innocent connotations, before it was taken over by the Nazis in Germany after the First World War. There was even a Swastika Cottage, beside the laundry in Shelbourne Road.

Brittain also owned a horse called Swastika, which was successful in shows at the nearby RDS. He put the swastika emblem on the chimney of his laundry and from the 1930s, the laundry's electric delivery vans were also emblazoned with the symbol. When the Nobel Prize-winning German author Heinrich Böll came to Ireland in the early 1950s, he was nearly knocked down by one of the Swastika Laundry vans, and, for a moment, thought that the Nazi propaganda machine was still active in Dublin. In 1939, two years after Brittain's death, the laundry changed its name to the Swastika Laundry (1912) to differentiate it from the Nazi Party in Germany, but the symbol remained in use.

The laundry was acquired by the Spring Grove Laundry Company in the late 1960s and in the early 2000s the site was sold for redevelopment. The old laundry was demolished in 2004 and replaced by the Oval office development, which stands in Shelbourne Road today. The old laundry chimney was left intact at the centre of this development, but without its swastika lettering.

Then: Swastika Laundry chimney. (*Image courtesy of Peter W. Brittain*)

Inset: Swastika Laundry van. (*Image courtesy of Peter W. Brittain*)

Now: Old Swastika Laundry chimney. (*Image by Hugh Oram*)

SWASTIKA
SWASTIKA
SWASTIKA
LAUNDRY DRY CLEANING

HAMMERSMITH WORKS

HAMMERSMITH WORKS ON Pembroke Road stood where Hume House is now located. The name dated back to when Richard Turner, an ironmonger turned ironsmith, moved to Ballsbridge and developed his ironworks there. The ironwork for many renowned buildings was made there, such as that for what was then Westland Row station, now Pearse station. Adjacent to the works, which were on an elaborate scale, Turner built his house, called Hammersmith House. Eventually, it became the principal's residence at the Veterinary College here, but the house was demolished in the mid-1950s to make way for an extension to the college.

About 1876, Turner's works moved to a new site, in North King Street, but William, son of Richard Turner, continued to live at Hammersmith House until his death in 1888. Then in 1891, George Crampton, a builder who lived in Herbert Avenue, Merrion, bought the site of the works and choose to continue the name Hammersmith Works. Crampton expanded considerably to become one of the largest building firms in the city and it built many of Ballsbridge's twentieth-century buildings. It remained at Pembroke Road until 1965, when it moved to new headquarters at Shelbourne Road, opposite the

Swastika Laundry. Crampton stayed there until 1996; the building was subsequently demolished and three new office blocks, called the Ballsbridge Centre, were built. Crampton moved to Simmonscourt Road and then to their present location, in Richview Office Park in Clonskeagh.

In 1965, Hammersmith Works were replaced by a new office block called Hume House, described in one review as 'one of the ugliest buildings in Ballsbridge', which had 'opened the floodgates for massive amounts of unsuitable office development in the area'.

Then: Hammersmith Works, Pembroke Road. (*Image courtesy of G. & T. Crampton*)

Now: Hume House, Ballsbridge, site of the Hammersmith Works. (*Image by Hugh Oram*)

JOHNSTON, MOONEY & O'BRIEN BAKERY, BALLSBRIDGE

FOR A CENTURY, the Johnston, Mooney & O'Brien bakery was one of the main employers in Ballsbridge, with up to 500 workers at its peak.

In the early nineteenth century, Duffy's calico and cotton mills on this site employed 400 and the firm had bleaching grounds on what was then the Forty Acres, now Herbert Park.

Duffy's mills had been built on the site of a sixteenth-century mill, one of several in the area, owned by Nicholas Duffy, who lived in an old castle here. He built the first wooden bridge over the River Dodder, which up until then, had been crossed by a ford. The subsequent stone bridge was named Ball' s Bridge, from which the district took its name. Once, what is now the Merrion Road outside the RDS was called Ball' s Bridge Road.

The bakery firm traces its origins back to 1835 but it took until 1889 for the three original firms to merge and create the present company, which then opened its bakery in Ballsbridge. A century ago, poor children from the district gathered outside the bakery with pillowcases, ready to be filled with broken bread.

One of the biggest developments on the site was the 1931/2 bakehouse, built by Cramptons. For many years, the bakery produced a wide selection of bread and confectionery, sold through its chain of retail shops, including one at the side of the bakery itself.

It also had a large fleet of horse-drawn bread carts; the manure was collected assiduously by gardeners in Ballsbridge and many other parts of the city. But in the 1950s, the firm was an early convert to green power when it replaced the carts with a fleet of battery powered delivery vans.

The bakery lasted in Ballsbridge until 1989 – the last manager of the bakery there, John Moloney, died recently – and it then moved to the old Downes bakery in Finglas; where it trades today. The site at Ballsbridge was sold to Telecom Éireann, the forerunner of Eircom, but changes in the ownership of the site led to much political controversy.

However, redevelopment eventually went ahead, creating many new apartments, an office block, Embassy House, which houses the *Irish Daily Mail* and the *Irish Mail on Sunday*, and the Herbert Park Hotel.

Next to the hotel stands the unoccupied building that once housed RTÉ Relays, which became Cablelink, then NTL and is now UPC. The cable company moved from here to the East Point Business Park in 2000. Before being used by the cable company, the building had housed the RTÉ Two television network.

Then: The Johnston, Mooney & O'Brien bakery, beside the river Dodder. (*Image courtesy of Ballsbridge, Donnybrook & Sandymount Historical Society*)

Now: The former site of Johnston, Mooney & O'Brien's bakery. Now occupied by Embassy House (an office block, on the left-hand side), the Herbert Park Hotel (right-hand side) and luxury apartments (rear). *(Image by Hugh Oram)*

IRISH HOSPITALS' SWEEPSTAKES

THE IRISH HOSPITALS' SWEEPSTAKES were once the largest employer Ballsbridge. Set up in 1930 to provide funding for Irish hospitals and profits for its promoters, its twin aims succeeded admirably. Over the following five decades, it became a byword for scandal and corruption because of its illegal sales in many countries around the world, including the UK and the USA. In the late 1930s, the draws were being staged in the Mansion House in Dublin, but just before the Second World War started, the Sweep was doing so well that it was able to move into its own brand-new headquarters in Ballsbridge. These were designed by Robinson & Keeffe and built by Crampton. The inset image shows the state-of-the-art canteen in the building, just after it opened, another, a later shot of the side of the two-storey building. The Sweepstakes building was constructed on the site of what was once of Ballsbridge's landmark sites, Ramsay's Royal Nurseries.

The Sweep gave employment, at its peak, to 5,000 clerical workers, many of them women, including widows who would not have been able to find work elsewhere. The profits of the Sweep also helped establish such factories as the Irish Glass Bottle Company in Ringsend and Waterford Glass. By the mid-1980s, the Sweep had been losing money for several years and it closed down, giving way to the National Lottery, which started in 1987. The vast Sweep premises were eventually demolished and new residential and

commercial accommodation was developed on the site, retaining the Sweepstake name.

Then: Irish Hospitals' Sweepstake building. (*Image courtesy of Ballsbridge, Donnybrook and Sandymount Historical Society*)

Inset: The canteen in the Irish Hospitals' Sweepstake building. (*Image courtesy of G. & T. Crampton*)

Now: Entrance to the Sweepstakes' development. (*Image by Hugh Oram*)

TRAM DEPOT

DIRECTLY ACROSS SHELBOURNE ROAD from Turner's Cottages was a tram depot, closed down in 1949, when the city's tram system ended. Soon it got an entirely different use. In 1950, the year that the Industrial Development Authority was set up, an entrepreneur called Stephen O'Flaherty acquired the franchise for Volkswagen cars for Ireland and Britain. He started assembling VW cars from parts shipped in from Germany. It was the first VW assembly plant outside Germany, and a VW car made in Shelbourne Road is now on display in the VW Museum in Wolfsburg, Germany. A well-known media personality, Derek Mooney of RTÉ, has a connection with this old VW factory; his father, Patrick, was an operative there. Parts arrived from Germany in crates and a short time later emerged as fully fledged VW Beetle cars, with their very distinctive lines.

The factory soon proved too small and in 1956 assembly was moved to larger premises on the Naas Road. The old factory was converted into a garage and showrooms for VW and Mercedes-Benz cars.

The original 1968 photograph shows Shelbourne Road in a very different light from the present-day street. Back in 1968, the tram depot, antecedents of the premises, can still be clearly seen, complete with old-fashioned petrol pumps. In recent years, the site has been so extensively redeveloped as a car showroom that it bears little resemblance to its origins.

Then: Ballsbridge Motors, Shelbourne Road. (*Image courtesy of Ballsbridge Motors*)

Now: Ballsbridge Motors, Shelbourne Road. (*Image by Hugh Oram*)

SIMMONSCOURT CASTLE

TODAY SIMMONSCOURT CASTLE is a gated development that stands at the top of Simmonscourt Road, 6.5 hectares with houses, apartments and the ruins of an old gate house. This is all that's left of the great castle that once stood on the site.

The history of Simmonscourt Castle goes back to the Smothe family, who occupied the land in the fourteenth century; the area was then called Smothescourt. It's said that the original castle was built during the fourteenth-century reign of King Edward III and then reconstructed in the sixteenth century.

After 1660, the castle was occupied by William, the 3rd Viscount Fitzwilliam and by the end of that century, the Nossam family were in residence, tenants of the owners, Christchurch cathedral. Originally, the first castle had become the property of the Priory of All Hallows, so throughout, Church authorities remained in ownership.

By about 1700, the castle was empty and falling into ruin. Today, only a small ruined block remains, probably a gate

house for that old castle and the history of the place is recorded on a large plaque beside the ruins. In the early eighteenth century, a house was built at Simmonscourt Castle and it was there that Arthur Forbes, the 2nd Earl of Granard, died in 1734. More building work was done on the estate during the Victorian era, including a second castle, then in the later twentieth century, new houses and apartments were built on the estate. Today, Simmonscourt Castle is an oasis of calm, as if it were in the middle of the country, yet as old signposts reminded visitors, it was only 1½ miles from the city centre.

Then: Simmonscourt Castle in the eighteenth century, now luxury apartments. *Image courtesy of Ballsbridge, Donnybrook and Sandymount Historical Society*)

Now: The remains of the old gate house at Simmons Court today. *(Image by Hugh Oram)*

CARISBROOKE HOUSE

THE HOUSE IN the old photograph was built in the 1860s and for many years, it was the home of the Lane Joynt family, well-known in Dublin legal circles. The 1911 census shows it occupied by William Russell Lane Joynt, aged fifty-six, Church of Ireland, his wife Nan, aged fifty-six, Roman Catholic, a daughter, Evelyn (twenty-four) and a son William (twenty-four) , both Roman Catholic, as well as two live-in domestic servants, Kate Farrell and Jane Byrne.

William Russell Lane Joynt's father (also William) was Mayor of Limerick in 1862 and Lord Mayor of Dublin in 1867. William Russell Lane Joynt was educated at Windermere in present day Cumbria, Bonn and at Trinity College, Dublin. He became a barrister. He was also a highly regarded philatelic expert and was keenly interested in shooting. At the 1908 London Olympics, he won a silver medal for shooting.

Rather ironically, in the immediate aftermath of the 1916 Easter Rising, British troop reinforcements were sent by sea to Kingstown, now Dun Laoghaire, and they marched into Dublin along Pembroke Road and Northumberland Road before being caught up in a ferocious and deadly ambush at Mount Street Bridge. Before they got to the bridge, however, the Sherwood Foresters freed Carisbrooke House, which had been occupied by three rebels, who between them had two rifles and one revolver.

In the 1940s, the house was bought by Charles J. Holohan, a solicitor in Lincoln Place, who was the father of John Holohan of the present-day Ballsbridge, Sandymount and Donnybrook Historical Society. Charles Holohan converted the house into flats, which were then let out. One resident who lived there subsequently was an elderly lady who had a menagerie of cats; the lady in question used to smoke 'Passing Clouds' cigarettes non-stop, lighting one from the previous cigarette.

In the mid-1960s, the house was demolished and replaced by the present-day eight-storey Carrisbrook House, built in an octagonal shape for a developer called Finbarr Holland. Among the occupants of the building today is the Israeli Embassy. In 2007, just as the Celtic Tiger boom was about to collapse, the building was bought for €46 million by a consortium led by Bernard McNamara and Gerry O' Reilly. When Goodbody's the stockbrokers was owned by AIB, it was based in Carrisbrook House, but in early 2010, the stockbrokers were bought by Fexco and the firm is now based at Ballsbridge Park, on the site of the old Sweepstakes' offices. (NB the old house was known as Carisbrooke House. Today, the modern building is known as Carrisbrook House).

Then: The original Carisbrooke House, Ballsbridge. *(Image courtesy of the Irish Architectural Archive)*

Now: The modern Carrisbrook House, at the corner of Pembroke Road and Norhumberland Road. *(Image by Hugh Oram)*